IN
HIS
LIGHT

Bill Davis

WINEPRESS  PUBLISHING

Printed in the United States of America.

Packaged by WinePress Publishing, PO Box 428, Enumclaw, WA 98022. The views expressed or implied in this work do not necessarily reflect those of WinePress Publishing. Ultimate design, content, and editorial accuracy of this work is the responsibility of the author.

ISBN 1-57921-336-7
Library of Congress Catalog Card Number: 00-109800

What people are saying about *In His Light*

"Thought provoking, inspirational, and God adoring."—Pastor Carl Nielsen, Bethal Lutheran Church, Santa Maria, CA

"I am truly touched by Gods grace as I read the message conveyed within these pages. This divine writing is proof of what can come through us if we only allow it. Upon my first visit with Bill I learned so much about him through his first hand accounts of miracles in progress. I am inspired by his ease with sharing his process of learning from each moment and each individual that he encounters. His gift of story and poem is uplifting in every sense."—Reverend Wendy K. McKenna

"Bill's poems bring spirituality plus enjoyment to me as I read them. He has been able to hear his inner voice from God and express it through his poetry so that everyone may partake in his understanding and wisdom."—Jane Morton, Homemaker

"Inspiring and uplifting, a great example of Gods amazing spirit expressed through words."—James Withrow, Juvenile Probation Officer

To my wife Kay, our children and grandchildren. They are the ones who have constantly encouraged me to write this book, and to an awesome God who gave me the material to write.

Contents

Introduction

I feel like I am standing in the light of God as He pours out His feelings, desires and love upon me and the whole human population. He encompasses the birds, animals and all the creatures of the universe. He made us for a relationship with Himself, but seldom do we take time to reach His way, to enjoy that love that only God can provide. He never forces His attention on us but He is always there when we need Him.

My prayer is that the contents of this book will give you a new outlook, a deep desire and a new love in your life that you never thought possible before.

THE GREATEST SMILE

Among my treasured thoughts I file
The image of the Lord's great smile
For there is something that I know
Recaptured in His face aglow.

It speaks of events just unfolding
And also thoughts newly molding
With logic so profoundly simple
That all is said with laugh and dimple.

It speaks of motives plain and clear
Expressed with glee or flood of tear
And tells of concerns not yet forming
And all my cares before their storming.

No self-awareness mars His smile
So perfect is the Lord's great style
It lets us know that all humanity
Had at first no trace of vanity.

It says to me when I am trusting
There've been many years of self adjusting
With a look of total purity
He radiates to me security.

But the thing that makes His smile outrageous
Is that it tends to be contagious
Despite our own predisposition
We wear a smile of recognition.

I find this simple interaction
The cause of boundless satisfaction
In drawing on an inner source
We wear a smile with lots of force.

~I am God's workmanship—Can you top that?~

Unnoticed

On life's busy thoroughfare,
We meet with angels unaware—
But we are too busy to listen and hear,
Too busy to sense that God is near.
Too busy to stop and recognize
The grief that lies in another's eyes.
Too busy to offer to help or to share.
Too busy to sympathize or care.
Too busy to do the things that we should,
Telling ourselves we would if we could—
But life is too swift and pace too great,
And we dare not pause or we may be late
For our next appointment which means so much,
We are willing to brush off the Lord's soft touch.
And we tell ourselves there will come a day
We will have more time to spend on the way—
But before we know it, life's sun has set
And we passed the Lord, but never met.
For as we hurry along life's thoroughfare,
We passed right by and were not aware
That within the sight of our very eye,
Unnoticed, the Lord passed right by.

~God makes each day in a special way; it's up to us what
we make of it.~

Chapter One
A Miracle I Have Seen

My First Miracle—Age 5

We lived on a farm in Nebraska, near the small town of Wilcox. It was a very hard time for everyone because of the Depression. Drought and dirt storms were prevalent, as well as a siege of grasshoppers, which eventually ate all of the crops and even the gardens.

My mother and father, two sisters and myself made up our family. One day my dear mother gathered us all together in the kitchen. She explained there was no food left in the house for us to eat. It was a cold winter day, and Christmas was coming soon. Mom had us all kneel on the old cold floor as she praised God. She praised Him for His goodness and care, and then explained to Him that the cupboards were empty. She concluded her prayer by thanking Him for all of our past blessings and said, "Amen, God." Suddenly, there came a knock on the door. My mother opened it, and as before, immediately thanked God. Standing at the door was a neighbor from some distance away;

who, by the way, had never been neighborly before. He looked at my mother and said, "I have just butchered a steer and thought I would give you a quarter of the beef. My wife sent these other groceries, for somehow, we felt you may need some help." My mother praised God for the rest of the day. As I passed her, I heard her say, "You always come through, somehow, someway." The complete faith of my mother was ingrained in my mind from this time forward. To this day, I know everything is possible with God.

The following poem was written as a result of this miracle of God, and I titled it, "My Mother's Faith."

MY MOTHER'S FAITH

My mother knelt on the floor to pray.
The weather was cold on this winter day.
Christmas was coming, soon to be here.
There was just no food; that was our fear.

As she knelt there, I heard my mother say,
"I praise you Lord, but we need you today.
The house is cold and the cupboard is bare.
We don't ask for much, and I know you care."

She thanked the Lord for the past blessings galore
And said, "Amen," then rose from the floor.
As we stood there, suddenly there was a knock on the door.
Mother opened it wide and thanked God as before.

For a man stood there with food aplenty
At least enough for one hundred and twenty.
My mother praised God the rest of the day,
"You always come through," I heard her say.

~There is a destiny that makes us one. No one goes there
alone: All that goes into the lives of others comes back
into our own.~

MY LITTLE MOTHER

My little mother, to her I bow
And doff my hat as I pass her by,
I reverence the furrows that mark her brow,
And the sparkling love-light in her eye.

My little mother—how often it seems
God chooses you for the greatest parts
You've had your share of joys and dreams
And probably also an aching heart.

But God knows well how you've done your best
And we all see you as someone great
My little mother, when you're put to the test
Never have we found you to be early or late.

~Never do our prayers go unanswered.~

MY MOTHER'S HANDS

My mother's hands were cool and fair.
They could do anything.
Delicate memories were hidden there
Like flowers in the spring.

When I was small and could not sleep,
She used to come to me
And with her hands upon my cheek,
How sure my rest would be.

For everything she ever touched
Was beautiful and fine.
The memories living in her hands
Would warm that sleep of mine.

Her hands remembered how we played,
At times in meadows and streams
And all the laughter, songs and shade
Just added to my dreams.

Swiftly through her strong fingers pass
memories of garden things.
I plunged my face in flowers and grass
And heard the sound of whirring wings.

One time she touched a cloud that kissed
Brown pastures bleak and far.
I leaned my cheek into her fist
And dreamed I became a star.

All this was very long ago,
And now I am grown.
The hands that lured my slumber so
I never can forget.

~Just close your eyes and meditate.~

MY FATHER

My father was a very strong man.
There was nothing he could not do.
He worked so hard to feed our clan.
The problems he faced were many and not a few.

He held his head above the rest
And put himself through every test.
His thoughts were good, his mind was clear.
Because of his strength he had no fear.

He challenged all who threatened his home.
His family came first without a moan.
He hid his tears from all of us,
But cry he did without a fuss.

He wept when an animal was put to sleep.
His whole body would shake, as he did weep.
He had compassion for man and beast
And helped everyone he could, to say the least.

His humor was known far and wide.
His stories were real and on the side.
Listeners came from near and far
And sat and listened in total awe.

He gave his life in those very last days
For the one he loved, it was his way.
He loved her so—that was very clear
So he gave his life without any fear.

God gave him a special place to rest,
For in every way he passed the test.
"Don't judge others by what you see.
Let God be the judge," that was his plea.

~Without God's direction, I can only just stand.~

My Grandfather

My grandfather was a mighty man—
A mighty man was he.
He stood so tall, with a wonderful tan.
Strong as an ox he seemed to be.

He cut the wood for our fires
And dug a well for our water.
He worked so hard and never seemed to tire.
His mind was clear and nothing seemed to matter.

One day his body came crashing down.
His legs were paralyzed.
I watched him struggle but no strength was found.
A wheelchair then had to be utilized.

I was only young, around about seven
When God took him home to heaven.
I missed him more than I can say,
But life goes on from day to day.

~Eternal life is what God sends; it goes on
and never ends.~

I Met the Master

When I was a child, I would have my
Mother read to me.
I would cry and cry because I was
Sad, you see.
There was David who slew Goliath
With a stone.
Then the battle of Jericho, where people
Yelled then would moan.
Then the lady who looked back
And turned into a pillar of salt.
It seemed to me so harsh
For just a minor fault.
Somehow my mind never let me past that place,
Until I met the Master face to face.

~I stopped and listened and heard God say, "I really love you; nothing can take that love away."~

CHILDHOOD

Do you ever think about the times
That filled your youthful years
With the joy of a light heart and happy dreams
And even those foolish little fears?

And all those many days
Of daring thrills and joys
That filled those carefree years of life
For all the girls and boys.

Each day of youth was much too short.
The nights were much too long,
For there was always more to do
That night would just prolong.

And every joy and promised thrill
Was mine to pursue
Without the wisdom and restraint
That older years accrue.

It was a time of true content,
In simple things of life—
With honest laughter, smiles and joys
That were not strained by strife.

A time when I explored and searched
And learned to love and play
And slept in peace, with faith and trust,
In God, each day by day.

~If you make a mistake and slip, He will pick you up
before you fall.~

TOGETHER

If life is full of challenge
And gives us outstretched wings,
Let's soar to higher places
And discover many things—
Together

If life reveals its message
To open eyes and ears,
Let's savor all the beauty
And conquer any tears—
Together

If life is meant for sharing
And time forever runs,
Let's find some hidden moments
And chase the setting sun—
Together

If life is meant for loving
And love is meant for two,
Let's never waste a moment
Nor even miss a cue—
Together

If life is ever lonely
As sometimes it seems be,
Let us recall the moments
When life placed you with me—
Together

~A light so bright the angel sang—a chorus so loud the heavens rang.~

THE ANSWER CAME

I walked along the path of life.
My heart was filled with hurt and strife.
Emptiness seemed to fill my being.
A way out I was not seeing.

And suddenly the answer came.
It came to my mind in the form of a name.
Ask God believing He'll set you free.
The answer is the same for you and me.

When you climb life's tallest ladder,
Take your faith along with you
And great will be your happiness
As your every dream comes true.

~There is a destiny that makes us one—No one goes
there alone: All that goes into the lives of others comes
back into our own.~

SOUL AND SPIRIT

The soul and the spirit go hand in hand
Always in step like a great marching band,
Creating their own want and desires,
With hearts of love burning as fire.

God formed a plan so large and great
That all mankind should celebrate.
He made it all for you and me.
Nothing can change that—don't you see?

God is the creator of all you can see.
He made it, I say, for you and me,
So worship Him, and give Him the glory,
And that is the word from this beautiful story.

~No one ever discovers the fullness or the expanse of His
greatness.~

TAKE A MINUTE

Take a minute to reflect
Upon the day just past.
Take a minute to collect
Sensations that will last.

Take a minute to enjoy
The precious here and now.
Take a minute to explore
The reasons why and how.

Take a minute to define
The subtleties of love.
Take a minute to observe
The mysteries from above.

Take a minute to extract
Some meaning from each other.
Take a special minute
Then another, and another.

~All real love comes from God, and not from each other.~

LOVE ONE ANOTHER

Where shall I go from Your spirit?
Or where shall I flee from Your presence?
If I took off on wings in the morning
And lived in the uttermost parts of the world,
Even then Your love and my love will meet.
And our love shall hold us together.

If we love one another, it penetrates
To the very core of our souls,
And our love is perfected in us
As our spirits relate to each other.
We are guided towards new and exciting experiences
And upward into new growth and happiness.

We who are of the trodden down must have courage—
Courage beyond the most common kind.
Let the problems of life linger longer
And be overcome, and become stronger.

Let those who persecuted with much bluster
Claim the world is theirs.
We shall hold steady and be not perturbed
About our very own affairs.

We have learned it is more than noise
That makes us strong and firm.
It is mainly in our hearts of love
That makes us large or small
Or stand above.

~Let God examine your heart—He loves you.~

Chapter Two

Miracles in Our World

MY SECOND MIRACLE—AGE 17

I was still in high school when World War II came about. I was drafted at a very young age and sent to the Pacific islands of New Guinea, Aitpe, Moratoi and Halmaherra and then onto the Philippines and Japan. We could never account for the many miraculous times that our lives were saved or kept from injury. When we invaded Luzon Island in the Philippines, the Japanese were waiting for us. They had captured the American long "Toms" or artillery canons in the hills and deluged us with shellfire. They fired a constant barrage on the beach where we were pinned down just off of the ships. I was in a shell crater with two other soldiers, one on each side of me. Suddenly, a very bright light appeared and I heard a voice say to me, "Go! Run, or you will be hit!" I told the two other soldiers what I had heard, but they would not leave. They did not believe my message. During a pause in the firing, I leaped out of the crater and ran toward the ocean and jumped into another crater. Later, I made my way back to the first crater to see what had become of the other two soldiers. Both men were badly hurt and later died. To my horror, the shell had hit and exploded right where I would have been lying.

The following two poems were written as a result of this experience. I have entitled them "Dear Lord" and "Dear Lord II."

DEAR LORD

Life's events don't always happen
Just as they are planned,
For the world this is a trying time—
I fully understand.

Dear Lord—Moments like the present
Seem to upset and confuse.
I'll try to give them my support
In any path they choose.

Dear Lord—I'll always listen with my heart.
I'll do what I can do.
I'll pray for better things to come,
If that's all right with You.

Dear Lord—You know our situation.
You're alert to life's demands,
But don't forget we are here,
And we're trying to understand.

~Though I walk in the midst of trouble—God will revive
me.~

DEAR LORD II

When life around us bubbles
In a most chaotic brew,
I can say in words right from the heart
I'm very glad there's You.

Dear Lord—For in this wacky world of ours
Through which we all are drifting,
Your influence is so very positive.
Your love is so uplifting.

Dear Lord—Bless those who are far away
And quiet all their sorrows.
Love the ones who miss them so
And bring a bright tomorrow.

~The best way to know God is love, for God is love.~

GOD HAS PROMISED

God has not promised
Skies always blue,
Flower strewn pathways
All our lives through.

God has not promised
Sun without rain,
Joy without sorrow,
Peace without pain.

But God has promised
Strength for each day,
Rest from your labor,
Light for your way.

And God has promised
Grace for trials,
Help from above,
Undying love—
Yes, God has promised.

~God has great plans for your life, even after death.~

TRUST HIM

The earth begins to rattle and everything does shake.
The mountains belch out lava
And we know we're in a quake.
Winds and rain join in the fray.

Fear grips the people everywhere.
They pray, "God, make it cease."
He waves His mighty hands right there
And calm gives all release.

To trust in Him this very day
For He alone is here to stay.
The trust you put in beast or man
Can ultimately ruin all your plan.

~What you can become, you are already.~

PRAY

When words begin to fail me,
A simple hug will do
To lighten all our burdens
And give us hope anew.

Heartaches can leave me speechless,
With nothing much to say.
Just Your being here speaks loudly,
And You always save the day.

Love can hurry up a healing.
You always light the way.
When words begin to fail me,
You tell me just to pray.

~The Lord will accomplish what concerns me.~

I Lost a Breath

Something happened in my heart
Just a very few breaths ago.
Its rhythm skipped and pained a bit
And caused me not to know.

I lost a breath; as I drew in,
A fleeting thought came through.
I heard you say—"Just trust Me,
And I'll keep loving you."

The warmth that it awakened,
The feelings that it stirred,
You nudged and gently told me
Something special had occurred.

For as I drew into my heart
Your image passing through,
I knew that I had lost a breath
And skipped a beat for You.

~The only end is in our mind; it's what we learned from
all mankind.~

OUR WORLD

I look across the hills
Where earth does touch the sky;
I see the deer and feel the thrills
From gentle breezes sailing by.

So much of nature lingers there;
So much of God I see
And marvel at the beauty in
The hills that fascinate me.

So, in my mind I am off and gone
On trails and magic ways.
I long to climb the hills again
With God on lovely days.

It's here I find a faith to keep
A peace and quiet real
Where nature seems to smile on me
And makes my dreams ideal.

The lovely sky that reaches down,
The fluffy clouds of white,
And then the moon so big and bright
And stars all shining light.

In His Light

I find it all a joy complete;
My heart is alive and free.
The miracles of life are mine
In the hills that beckon me.

~The world is round, and the place which may seem like
the end may also be the beginning.~

THANK YOU, LORD

Please listen to me as I pray—
I thank You, Lord, for this great day.
I have noticed many wondrous things—
The smallest life, the bird that sings.

God, grant us the strength to do
Some needed service here,
The wisdom to be brave and true
And the gift of vision clear.

That as each task comes to me
Some purpose we may plainly see.

God teach me to believe that I
Am surrounded by a host,
Who protects us where we stand or lie,
Where we are needed most.

That at last, if we do well,
Our humble services then will tell.

God, grant us faith to stand on guard
Uncheered without fan fare alone,
And see the gain, no matter how hard,
Of our services to Your throne.

~Whatever our tasks, let this be our creed: We are here
on this earth to fill a need.~

Fly, Spirit, Fly

My joyous, excited spirit wants to fly
Until I can reach the summit of the sky,
Reaching into space for a comfortable seat,
I'll pluck a star that can't be beat,
Forming it into a ring of fire so bright
The reflections will blind you in the sunlight.

Dazzled and forced to shade your eyes,
For the beautiful brilliance will bring great sighs.
For peace and joy fill your very life.
Love ends all your misery and strife.
Our story shall be told through all the pages,
Passed on again and again through many ages.

How do you find peace, joy and song?
What is it we've done that seems so wrong?
You failed to reach for a higher plateau.
It's there for you too, if you want to know.
Throw your head back and gaze with a beautiful smile
Over the heads of others for at least a mile.
Keep your thoughts on the great and splendid things
As your mind forms an image of your special ring.
Thought is supreme; your mind will create
All things you desire before it's too late.
So it's yours for the taking; by now, you know.
It's peace, joy and love for mind, body and soul.

~The idols of the nations are of silver and gold.~

PEACE

Our body has its mortal fears,
Seeing even the sunlight disappear.
When dusk draws in, you feel your breath
And wonder then, and ask, "What is death?"

And your spirit, with a keener sight,
Has knowledge direct from the infinite.
It's a bridge across a quiet stream,
An open door beyond a dream.

~No one, O God, is Your equal.~

THE MIGHTY OCEAN

The ocean crashed
With an awesome roar,
Hurling endless torrents at the shore.
Its mighty force shook the land
And ground tall cliffs into tiny sand.

But at the thundering edge of doom,
Amidst the turmoil,
Small flowers bloom.

They have no concern for wind or tide—
Their frail petals open wide
And cast a fragrance over the air
As if the loud sea was never there.

~No mistake—it was God's creation.~

Chapter Three

A Miracle of Faith

My Third Miracle—Age 23

I was just out of the service, married, and living in North Platte, Nebraska. We had three wonderful children; Bill, the oldest, Mike, and then Mary, the baby. I was working on the railroad as a switchman in the Union Pacific yards and had a second job with the State Highway Division. Sleep was a problem for me. Our baby Mary had a terrible asthmatic condition that caused us to rush her to the hospital on almost a weekly basis. She needed to be put into an oxygen tent to help her breathe. The doctors finally came to the conclusion that the best thing for Mary would be for us to move out of this area and find someplace that would not trigger these attacks. The doctors warned us that the constant pressure caused by these attacks would damage Mary's heart. We agreed to move, but we did not know where to go to make Mary better. Our first move was to Grand Junction, Colorado, but Mary's attacks continued. After several months, we decided to move again. This time to the

Bay Area in California. One night, soon after our arrival in California, Mary again became very ill. We rushed her to Kaiser Hospital in Oakland, where they treated her with oxygen tents and wet sheets. The doctors told us she might not make it.

We prayed constantly for our little girl, while she lay for several days lifeless in the hospital bed. Suddenly, Mary opened her eyes, looked up and smiled at us. It was not long before she was bouncing on the bed and playing. From that day she has not suffered from another attack. It was a miracle.

The following poem was written as a result of this miracle. I have entitled it, "Never Alone" because my family and I were never alone throughout this trying time.

NEVER ALONE

We never carry our burdens alone,
For God is our Father, and we are His own.
There is no problem we cannot meet
If we lay them all at His holy feet.

No matter how big man's problems are
God's answers are very definitely more,
For always God's giving is greater by far
Than what man can think to ever ask for.

~I am an optimist. It does not seem much use being
anything else.~

GIVE THANKS

It's thanks I give for so many things,
Yes, thanks on this and every day
For all of the blessings that God brings
Everyday in so many ways.

I give thanks for life, for health,
For home, for food and family, too.
I count that my greatest wealth
Is in friends that are true blue.

I give thanks for God's hand
That holds me this day.
For my worship He understands;
He has taught me so much,
But, above all, He taught me to pray.

I give thanks for so many things,
And I try the best I can
To be worthy of all that God brings
And serve Him as a faithful man.

~We never become truly spiritual by sitting down and
wishing to become so.
You must undertake something so great that you
cannot accomplish it unaided.~

GOD KNOWS BEST

Our God knows what is best for us,
So why should we complain?
We always want the sunshine,
But He knows there must be rain.

We love the sound of laughter
And the merriment of cheer,
But our hearts would lose their tenderness
If we never shed a tear.

Our Father tests us often
With suffering and with sorrow.
He tests us not to punish
But to help us meet tomorrow.

For growing trees are strengthened
When they withstand the storm.

God never hurts us needlessly.
He never wastes our pain,
For every loss He sends to us
Is followed by rich gain.

And when we count our blessings
That God so freely sent,
We will find no cause for murmuring
And no time to lament.

For our God loves His children
and to Him all things are plain.

So whenever we are troubled
And when everything goes wrong,
It is just God working in us
To make our spirits strong.

~Our knowledge comes from learning, and all wisdom
comes from God.~

A Tiny Bird

I never know what it may be
That attracts me to a bird or tree,
But hummingbirds God specially made
To show His love when we have prayed.

Their beauty is beyond compare.
As you watch them go here or there,
Their colors come from angels passing through
And drop their colors from heaven blue.

I have learned to watch and then
Praise God for what we enjoy again.
A tiny bird that has touched our hearts—
Thank You, Lord, for their small parts.

~When you climb each step of life's ladder, take your
faith along with you.~

I KNOW

When asked where does the Lord reside,
I fondly said, "Inside, inside."
When thoughts of places I have lived
Welled up within, I softly cried.

When asked where do these feelings start,
I then replied "The heart, the heart."
I know their penetrating force
When finally I must depart.

In spaces where my memories roam,
I conjure up the home, the home—
That state of mind that rests upon
A special portion of the loam.

What consecrates the dwelling so—
As hallowed place I know, I know.
It is who resides within that place
And finds the needed space to grow.

~It seems like time does fly, and then it stops only to start
again.~

SHARING

*I enjoy the times when I am with You.
I'm happy when we are talking.
I value all the things we do,
The quiet moments when walking.*

*So many things are better shared,
And I am so glad that we
Find such complete fulfillment
In each other's company.*

*There is more to life when You are around.
You make me feel alive.
There is nothing to withhold from You.
With You I can survive.*

*I am able to explore my thoughts,
Relax in freedom found.
The confidence I feel is
Reassuring and profound.*

*The moments we are together
Are such special ones to me.
Because I sense that we exist
In spiritual harmony.*

~God said, "Your life I have spoken for—walk with me or
close the door."~

SUCH AS YOU

For such as you, I do believe,
Spirits their softest carpets weave
And spread them out with gracious hands
Wherever you walk, wherever you stand.

For such as you, of scent and dew,
Spirits their rarest nectar brew
And where you sit and where you sup
Pour beauty's elixir in your cup.

For all day long, like other folk,
You bear the burden, wear the yoke,
And yet when I look in your eyes this eve,
You are lovelier than ever, I do believe.

~Dreams come often and dreams come late. Dreams
sometimes come when you meditate.~

MY CHILDREN

My children are the best you see—
How could it not be plain to me
Each one is full of love and care
And that is only being fair.

All are special, in their own way
God placed in them a shining ray
They place God first, before you and me
Just as He asked, don't you see.

Their lives are blessed each single day
They know Him along their way
Their families show love without reserve
And are always ready to help and serve.

~My children are God's children adopted by
us for awhile~

A Little Bird

The tree limbs sway when the winds blow,
Yet the little birds sing in spite of the flow.
I like to believe that as a man,
I can do as well as a little bird can,
But you must have faith, in the rightness of things
To put yourself out on just feathers and wings
And sing when there seems to be nothing there
But cold winds and empty air.
Teach me little bird to go to the top of the tree
Of my mind and sing your song inside of me.

~Lessons can be learned from God's smallest creation.~

BEGIN WITH GOD

Watch the spiders—how they spin,
And take a lesson with a grin.
God sends the thread for a web begun;
The words of the proverbs seem to run.

So, whatever it is you hope to win,
Create or accomplish, or just begin,
The fruitful harvest for which you pray
Is locked in the seed that you sow today.

The joyous journey you long to make
Begins with the first firm step you take,
So lift your eyes to your special star;
Step out boldly where you are
Beginning the task you long to do.
God will help you see it through.

~When you pray and ask God for a gift, and be grateful if
He sends not diamonds, gold and riches, but the love of
real, true friends.~

Birthdays Are a Gift from God

Where does the time go in its endless flight?
Spring turns to fall, and day to night.
Birthdays come, and birthdays go.
Where they go, we do not know.

God, who planned our life on earth,
Gave our mind and body birth
And then enclosed a living soul
With heaven as the spirit's goal

He has given man the gift of choice
To follow that small, inner voice
That speaks to us from year to year,
Reminding us there is nothing to fear.

For birthdays are a stepping stone
To endless joys, yet unknown,
So fill each day with happy things
And may your burdens all take wings.

Fly away and leave behind—
Great joy of heart and peace of mind.
For birthdays are the gateway to
An endless life of joy for you.

If you pray from day to day,
He will show you the truth and the way.

~Birthdays go—we know not where.~

OUR FRIENDS

We cannot count our friends, nor say
How fortunate we are each day by day.
Every one of us has friends that we
Have yet to meet and really know.
They come from near and far,
Wherever they may be,
And brighten up our life, leave us with a glow;
They help to light our path with cheer
Although they pass so seldom here.

We cannot guess how large the debt
We owe to friends we have just met.
We only know, from day to day
That we discover here and there
How they have tried to smooth our way
And sense how much they really care.
They passed along and left behind
Their friendly gift for us to find.

~Birthdays are a new start in life eternal.~

A KIND FRIEND

One never knows
How far life and time goes.
One never sees
How far a smile of friendship flees.
Down through the years
Those we care for disappear.

One kindly word
The souls of many here has stirred.
Man goes his way
And tells with every passing day
Until life ends,
"Once unto me he was my friend."

We cannot say
What lips are praising us today.
We cannot tell
Whose prayers ask God to guard us well.
But kindness lives
Beyond the memory of him who gives.

~Thank God for your real friends.~

Chapter Four

The Miracle That
Could Not Happen—Did

MIRACLE FOUR

Six months after my family and I joined the neighborhood church, I had a wonderful experience that once again brought me closer to our Lord. Late one evening my telephone rang; it was my brother-in-law telling me about his sister who was in intensive care in the local hospital. His hopes of her healing were diminishing, and he was at the point of reaching to anything or anyone who could help. He asked me if I would call my pastor and ask him to visit his sister and pray for her. I enthusiastically agreed, knowing that this part of my family had never been close to the Lord. I immediately called my pastor and arranged to meet him at the hospital. When we arrived, she was deep in a coma. My pastor walked up to her, held her hand and began to pray. He then asked me to talk to her. I was feeling very disappointed because of the coma—I believed she would not hear us and we would be of no help. My pastor encouraged me to keep talking to her and to believe that the Lord would work through us and get His word to her. "Marion, Marion," I said, "I hope you can hear us. We want to tell you about the Lord." Suddenly, Marion awoke, looked up at us and said that she had been listening. And with that, she turned her head, closed her eyes and slipped back into a coma.

The Lord did not take her that evening, and she began to get stronger. A few days passed, and the Pastor and I went to visit her in the hospital. When I arrived, several of her family members were there. The Pastor asked Marion if she remembered my visit that night in the intensive care unit. She said she did, and proceeded to tell everyone about how she met the Lord that evening. That same evening, after I arrived home, the telephone rang. It was my brother-in-law. He told me that the Lord had taken Marion home just a few minutes ago. This miracle of the Lord had such a profound impact on my life. I understood that Marion died a believer only because of the time we shared with her in intensive care. This proved to me that nothing has ever been impossible with God; even on your dying day, you can be changed by a miracle.

MIRACLES

Miracles seem to be all around,
Within our sense of sight and sound,
Proclaiming to all who are doubting men
That God is all things alive again.

I desire to be always aware
In everything I do
That our knowledge comes from learning
And all wisdom comes from You.

Help us all to realize
There is untold strength and power
When we seek our God and find Him
In our meditation hour.

~Solutions are God's specialty—ask Him.~

WHERE TO PRAY

Any place is one for prayer.
I need not travel anywhere.
All I need is a moment's pause
To tell God my specific cause.

A stop sign, a sudden hush,
Between a conversation stream—
Just glance away, or use a brush
The time it takes to change your beam.

Now every little interlude
I gratefully applaud,
Aware each one has just renewed
My centeredness in God.

~Remember any place is the right place to pray and thank
Him.~

THE LITTLE THINGS

The little things I love about you
Are the most worthwhile.
A friendly conversation or your usual happy smile,
The willingness to always share
Is how I know you really care.
Sometimes the reason may seem quite small
But little things mean the most of all.
He will heal our bodies, souls and spirits.

~Light up your world with a smile.~

GOD'S PLAN

God made a plan so large, so great,
But who of us can possibly relate?
He separated the darkness and the light
And called it day, and also night.

He made us all in His own image—
Brothers and sisters in God's lineage.
Fellowship was His deep desire,
Our time for Him just seems to expire.

A little time here and sometimes there—
I think He feels we may not care.
Yet His love is there for everyone
From early morn to setting sun.

He waits and waits for us to come,
To spend the time, He does with some.
His plan for us is greater still,
For in it we are in His will.

Let's spend some time from each twenty-four hours
To be with Him, and witness His powers.
He loves us all, without any reservation
And promises us eternal preservation.

~When you climb each step of life's ladder, take your
faith along the way.~

I Am with You

If we listen, we shall hear
Words of assurance in our ear.
The decision today is your choice.
"I have prepared you," comes His voice.
Quietly he whispers, "I am always with you
My child, I shall never leave you.
Before you can call, I will answer.
Before you hear, it has been done.
In this world you shall have trials—
Mountains in your paths for endless miles.
I am there to teach you the way,
For I overcame the world
And am here to stay."

~Polish your friendship with God; keep it free of tarnish.~

GOD KNOWS BEST

I watched some angels passing by
And then a rainbow arched in the sky—
Wonderful thoughts raced through my mind.

Your presence here has blessed us all.
Come back again, and please do call.
The blessings flow to us within.
I am glad to say you are my kin.

I hate to see you leave, I say,
But when you go, your hearts will stay.
God knows the best about all of this,
But let me say, you will be missed.

~Allow others to see God in your life.~

WAIT FOR THE ANSWER

Your answers will come,
Just wait upon Me.
Get on with your life—
I'm in control, you see.
You're doing just fine,
And what you're doing is right.
Just leave it to Me;
That's half of the fight.

We all need to practice patience.
Abide in faith

We were told by a higher power
That this coming year will be the hour.
We've been given all we'll ever need—
The desire and the will to succeed.

Nothing can ever fail us now,
For what is to be, will be somehow.
The problems will come and then fade away,
So abide in faith, for you're here to stay.

~Try turning the light on in another—a friend is a gift of
God.~

HERE TO STAY

O Lord, our Lord,
Majestic is Your name.
When I consider Your heavens,
Your work is all the same.

The work of Your hands,
The moon and the stars,
The water and the land,
From both near and afar—

You labored until the earth was made
And man and woman were here to stay.
Your plan was perfect and so well laid.
We accept Your gift until judgment day.

~When you pray and ask God for a gift, be ever grateful if
He sends not diamonds, gold, or riches, but the love of
real, true friends.~

PATH TO ME

You've scanned the distance
In vain, to see
The lighted narrow path
That leads direct to Me.

I recognize your footsteps.
Your voice is clear to Me.
Come rest your weary head
Upon My giant knee.

My hand shall soothe your brow
As I fill your heart with peace.
Let your thoughts be these of love,
And receive a full release.

Angel wings shall appear upon you.
You shall soar so very high.
You shall mount up on wings as eagles—
There's no limit in the sky.

Look up—My voice is shouting.
The earth is so very vast.
Look up—you are a child of God,
And all that is, will soon be past.

~Feel the awe and wonder of God's creation.~

GOD'S LOVE

I sat by the window last night
And watched the sky so beautiful and light.
I marveled at the stars way up so high
And wondered when God would take me, with a sigh.

I searched my mind all through the night,
Not knowing for sure if I was right.
I sought for answers from God above.
He said to me, "It's all based on love."

Love one another with an earnest heart.
Step back and look, then make a new start.
True love is not here today and gone tomorrow—
That only results in misery and sorrow.

God's love is all powerful and everywhere present.
Love is fulfilling and certainly heaven sent.
Love is like a warm blanket around you today.
Love permeates you and glows like a ray.

Your answer will come; just wait upon Me.
Go on with your life. I am in control you see.
You're doing fine, and what you're doing is right.
Just leave the rest to Me with all of My might.

~Today, cultivate and appreciate the beauty in nature.~

RISE ABOVE IT

Like an eagle soaring,
We too can rise above.
No matter what befalls us,
God will hold us in His love.

Soar to heights above the clouds.
Look back to earth below us.
Our peace and joy abounds
And our God is whom we trust.

The moon and stars come out again
And night and darkness reign.
We feel so safe in His great arms,
And we witness all His charms.

~Allow love and peace to prevail.~

COMPANIONSHIP

I walk the path almost every day,
A path so familiar, it's a friendly way.
Precious memories come again;
I love to sing their sweet refrain.

This quiet time brings healing power,
And I let God's love command the hour;
Then soon I am renewed, made whole—
A whole new outlook lifts my soul!

Though I have much yet to let go,
A lot more memories must grow.
They need this time to talk and talk
And share deep longings while I walk.

Dear God, help me that I may live
Less to forget and more to forgive.
May all my thoughts with you now find
Companionship in heart and mind.

~Let your heart overflow with gratitude, and your joy will
overflow.~

LET'S MEDITATE

I stand at a crossroad this day—
I want to go but I must stay.
The work is not done,
And the hour is so late—
Why is it people cannot communicate?

Our God has something important to say.
He has tried and tried in many a way.
Open your mind; be quiet and wait.
That's what it means to meditate.

Let your energy run with an even flow.
The message shall come and you shall know
What God has to say this very day.
Miracles will happen along the way.

~God's standards lend to success—always.~

SHARE WITH ME

Share with me Your great big world—
Reveal to me Your thinking.
Tell me when Your spirits soar,
And tell me when I'm sinking

Share with me Your every move—
Permit me to explore
Your love and admiration;
Let me know You to the core.

~Teach me to do Your work.~

I Believe

A long time I looked into the night
And felt the cold with a real bite,
I stood there as the clouds drift by,
Hiding the moon up there so high.

Sharing the universe and the infinite depth,
Feeling God and His eternal breath,
Knowing it is all true,
I have this feeling—
I believe it all; it is all unchanging.

~The angels sing Your fame.~

God's Promise

God did not promise sun without rain,
Light without darkness or joy without pain—
He only promised us strength for this day
When the darkness comes and we lose our way.

God did promise to see us through
Whether darkness, pain, hunger or flu—
His hand is there to lift you up
When the trials come, and you must look up.

"Have faith," He said, "as a mustard seed,
And I'll move a mountain to intercede—
Hand in hand we'll go all the way
From here to eternity, where forever we'll stay."

~By the Word of God the heavens were made. Incline
your ears, and listen to what He said.~

Chapter Five

Relaxing in God's Light

LAUGH AT LIFE

Whatever the task and whatever the risk,
Wherever fresh the air,
The funny person with sunny ways
Is sure to be laughing there.

There are those who fret;
There are those who dream,
Those making the best of it,
But whatever the trials or hardship they face
Or burning thirst in a desert place,
There is always one, by the good Lord's grace,
Who is making a jest of it.

They travel wherever others go,
And they leave no sorrow behind them.
The need for smiles and laughter, too,
In the ranks of sadness you'll find them.

When some are weary and sick and faint
With problems that are choking,
We dance there with our spirits gay,
And tint with gold what was drab and gray
And into the gloom of the night and day,
We scatter our mirthful laughter.

How much depends on we who stirred
The souls of people with cheerful word
And kept them brave by a jest absurd
And brightened their days with laughter.

~I take His hand without fear, for He brought me here.~

WHEN I AM ALONE

Strange thoughts come when I'm alone.
It's then I question the why and where
And what is right and what is fair
In the roll of life where my soul has grown.
It's then in the quiet I talk with the Lord
About how to start and end my days
And what should I blame and what should I praise.
His answers come as straight as a board.

When I have been with the busy throng,
It's nice to retreat to the silent hours—
Low voices whisper of higher powers,
And I catch the strain of some far off song.
The sham fades and my eyes can see,
Not the man I am in the days hot strife
And the greed and grind of a selfish life,
But the soul of the man I am to be.

I feel the throbbing of life divine
And catch the glimpse of a greater plan.
I question the purpose and work of man.
In the hours of silence, my mind grows fine.
I seek to learn what is kept unknown.
I turn from self and its garb of clay
And dwell on the soul and higher way—
Strange thoughts come when I'm alone.

~God will not leave me alone, so I reach and take His hand.~

THE ONES WE LOVE

We never lose the ones we love,
For even though they are gone,
Within the hearts of those who care,
Their memory lingers on.

It's very hard to bear the loss
Of someone dear to you,
And though there is so little now
That I can say or do,

I find comfort in the thought
My loss is shared today
By those who cared about you more
Than words could ever say.

~I do not know the path—He does.~

I Miss You So

Life may sometimes be a short span.
You may live it to the fullest
Or maybe just the most you can,
For inside you feel so very blessed.

But whether life is short or long
Or for all of eternity,
You feel the rights will offset the wrongs
And freedom comes completely.

Life sometimes lays a heavy load
You think you cannot bear,
But love and you go down the road
And find strength to spare.

Love lifts you up to new-found peaks
On giant and mighty wings.
When life is happiest and must speak,
Love is the song it sings

The end of life may be only a new start.
How can anyone really know?
But my heart aches, for we're apart,
And I terribly miss you so.

~He alone knows what we are most needing.~

We Lost—We Gained

We have walked together
Through the hour of death,
And even though we lost, we gained.
Each day began with new hope
And baited breath,
But we reached new spiritual plateaus
As our eyes were tear-stained.

Our emotions were torn to new highs and lows
As the days and nights were so very long,
But our spirits met and challenged our vows
To be faithful until end
Right or wrong.

So we took up the battle to win anyway
With positive thinking and great faith aloft,
But the battle was lost, so what can I say?
We were sure that we won, but we lost.

Our love reached out and grew and grew
To new heights we had never reached before,
So our love for Him increased, it's true.
And so, even though we lost, we gained,
Yes, gained even more.

~More than hearts can imagine or minds comprehend.~

BLESSED ASSURANCE

Though I may walk in valleys deep in shade,
My heart made sad by death where lie my hopes,
I still may face the future unafraid,
For God will clasp the hand that blindly grasps.

His rod of principle is in my hand
To banish doubts and make my pathway free;
His staff of understanding gives command
Of certainty that guides and comforts me.

Then sure I am that goodness shall abide;
His mercy shall be mine in richest store—
That in God's house I may reside
In peace and perfect bliss forevermore.

~The fruit of God's love is there for all.~

PLEASE DON'T CRY

Please don't cry when I die.
I was only passing through.
This never was my home for long.
It was only time to meet with you.

Have a laugh and a party too.
There's cause to rejoice for I love you.
Life must go on from day to day,
And soon you'll come with me to stay.

Life never ends because of death.
It's just a pause to hold your breath.
The best is surely yet to come—
When we meet God it will be fun.

His promises are as good as ever.
Our God has plans; He is so clever.
The rest of life will be without strife,
For He promised us all eternal life.

~Grief can take care of itself, but to get full value of joy,
you must have somebody to divide it with.~

THIS IS ME

Each time you look up in the sky
And see the clouds go drifting by
Or touch a flower, a leaf or tree,
It's all God whispering: "This is Me . . ."

Whenever it rains on mother earth
And all of nature then gives birth,
The sun comes out for all to see.
Yes, it's God whispering: "This is Me . . ."

The angels sing and shout for joy
When a girl is born, or even a boy—
Daily miracles that you always see,
For it's God whispering: "This is Me . . ."

~His greatness exceeds life.~

WHEN TIME STOOD STILL

I stood alone on the brink of my life
And viewed the joy, the love, the strife.
The picture changes from day to day.
What I see now is not here to stay.

It's always changing; it will not last.
What's happening now,
Has just gone past.
Time will not stop; it's just for today,
So enjoy your life; it will not stay.

But One who is there
From the very start
Will love you and guide you
And make you a part
Of a world so big. He made it
When time stood still.

~Who can doubt that we exist only to love? We live not a
moment exempt from its influence.~

NEVER ALONE

We never carry our burdens alone,
For God is love, our Father,
And we are His own.
There's no problem we cannot meet
If we lay them all at His holy feet.
No matter how big man's problems are,
God's answers are very definitely more,
For always God's giving
Is greater by far
Than what man can think
To ever ask for.

~He alone knows what we need.~

ANGELS WATCH

Silently the angels hover over us
On a nearby hill, by our side.
They are thus.
No matter where we go, they are there,
Protecting, helping, doing God's work
Everywhere.

They are always there.
It is like drinking water
When I am thirsty.
It is like standing on a hilltop,
My heart bursting.
It is like watching the ocean's power.
It is like being on the Eiffel Tower.

I close my eyes and they are still there;
I open them and am fully aware.
It is like being with someone I love,
For I know I am watched
By someone above.

~I am watched by someone above.~

Look Up

Look to the sky
Beyond the furthest star
And then look beyond—
That's where we are.

We wait, we watch, we listen—
Lest the hours shall slip away,
Yet be not dismayed or puzzled,
For we are where you will be someday.

We see every shadow
And every light upon the path.
We hear your voice so clearly now,
So we send you love, not wrath.

Look up, it is I that is calling.
You shall be accounted for.
Have no fear that you are falling,
For it is you that I adore.

And gaze upon the sky in peace—
Observe the balance as clouds increase.
Look to the sky for every clue,
For Thomas doubted, just like you.

~There is a touch of His great care in all creation—
everywhere.~